World's Weirdest Plants

Banyan Trees Strangle Their Host!

By Janey Levy

Gareth Stevens Publishing

Please visit our website, www.garethstevens.com. For a free color catalog of all our high-quality books, call toll free 1-800-542-2595 or fax 1-877-542-2596.

Library of Congress Cataloging-in-Publication Data

Names: Levy, Janey, author.
Title: Banyan trees strangle their host! / Janey Levy.
Description: New York : Gareth Stevens Publishing, [2020] | Series: World's weirdest plants | Includes index. | Summary: "Banyan trees are fig trees that are often known by another name: strangler figs. And there's a good reason for that. The seeds land on other trees and sprout there, sending down roots that slowly strangle the host tree."– Provided by publisher.
Identifiers: LCCN 2019026606 | ISBN 9781538246313 | ISBN 9781538246320 (library binding) | ISBN 9781538246306 (paperback) | ISBN 9781538246337 (ebook)
Subjects: LCSH: Banyan tree–Juvenile literature.
Classification: LCC QK495.M73 L48 2020 | DDC 583/.648–dc23
LC record available at https://lccn.loc.gov/2019026606

First Edition

Published in 2020 by
Gareth Stevens Publishing
111 East 14th Street, Suite 349
New York, NY 10003

Designer: Katelyn E. Reynolds
Editor: Abby Badach Doyle

Photo credits: Cover, p. 1 Arga Prasetya/Shutterstock.com; cover, pp. 1–24 (background) Conny Sjostrom/Shutterstock.com; cover, pp. 1–24 (sign elements) A Sk/Shutterstock.com; p. 5 Amit kg/Shutterstock.com; p. 7 Andrei Minsk/Shutterstock.com; p. 9 (center banyan tree) Parrot Ivan/Shutterstock.com; p. 9 (canopy) Moolkum/Shutterstock.com; p. 9 (leaves and figs) manistock/Shutterstock.com; p. 9 (branches) Mazur Travel/Shutterstock.com; p. 9 (roots) Ong.thanaong/Shutterstock.com; p. 11 Amornnat Malai/Shutterstock.com; p. 13 f2.8/Shutterstock.com; p. 15 Somchai Siriwanarangson/Shutterstock.com; p. 17 Frank Bienewald/LightRocket via Getty Images; p. 19 (main) Thipwan/Shutterstock.com; p. 19 (inset) sudipkunu/Shutterstock.com; p. 21 Vladimir Melnik/Shutterstock.com.

Printed in the United States of America

CPSIA compliance information: Batch #CW20GS : For further information contact Gareth Stevens, New York, New York at 1-800-542-2595.

CONTENTS

Words in the glossary appear in **bold** type the first time they are used in the text.

BEHOLD THE BANYAN TREE

Trees give us many kinds of fruit, including apples, oranges, and figs. One type of fig tree is the banyan (BAN-yuhn) tree. But it's not an ordinary tree—it's known as a strangler fig because of how it grows. Seeds land on other trees. As the seeds **sprout**, they send down roots that strangle, or choke, the **host** tree. How weird is that?

The banyan tree is famous for its great size and many uses. You'll learn more about this strange tree inside this book.

SEEDS OF KNOWLEDGE

The largest banyan tree alive today covers such a huge area that 20,000 people can stand under it!

The scientific name of the banyan tree is *Ficus benghalensis.*

HOME AND HABITAT

You'll have to travel a long way to see banyan trees in their native home. They're found in the Asian countries of India, Pakistan, and Bangladesh. The banyan is the national tree of India. There, it is known as the wish-fulfilling tree.

Banyan trees grow in tropical forests throughout these three countries. Tropical forests are found in warm areas near the equator (ee-KWAY-tuhr). What's the equator? It's an imaginary line around Earth that's the same distance from the North and South Poles.

Where to Find Banyan Trees

Here are some of the places where you can find banyan trees.

THE PLANT AND ITS PARTS

The banyan tree doesn't look like any other tree you've seen. It's a huge, wide tree that seems to have many **trunks**. But what look like trunks are actually roots sent down from the tree's branches into the ground. These **aerial** (AIR-ey-uhl) or **prop** roots grow thick over time.

Broad, shiny, and oval green leaves fill the banyan tree's **canopy**. These large leaves can be almost 8 inches (20 cm) long! And since the banyan tree is a fig tree, it of course has figs.

SEEDS OF KNOWLEDGE

The largest banyan tree in the world is the Great Banyan Tree, located near Kolkata, India. It covers 4.7 acres (1.9 ha). That's far larger than the average Walmart store!

The Banyan Tree

canopy

leaves and figs

branches

roots

A single large banyan tree can look like a small forest.

THE FRUIT AND ITS HIDDEN FLOWERS

Banyan trees are different from other fruit trees you may have seen. Why? You never see flowers on them. If you know how fruit trees make fruit, you know that usually flowers come first. Bugs, birds, or bats **pollinate** the flowers. Then, the flowers produce fruit. That's not what happens with banyans!

Figs—banyan trees' fruit—are actually hollow, fat stem tips that have flowers *inside* them! How do those hidden flowers get pollinated? Well, that's the story for the next chapter.

SEEDS OF KNOWLEDGE

Since banyan trees' flowers are hidden, many early societies believed the trees didn't have flowers at all.

Inside each fig are hundreds of tiny **male** and **female** flowers. Male flowers have pollen and female flowers have seeds.

JUST ONE KIND OF WASP

Only one species, or kind, of small wasp can pollinate banyan trees. A female enters a fig through a tiny hole, which closes behind her. She carries eggs and pollen to pollinate the flowers. She dies after laying her eggs.

After the eggs hatch, or break open, the new males and females **mate**. The males chew a hole in the fig. The females leave through this hole. They fly off to find new figs, carrying pollen and eggs with them. And the **cycle** starts again

SEEDS OF KNOWLEDGE

The male wasps are born inside a fig and die after mating with the females. That means they live their entire life inside a fig. That's really weird!

The female wasp loses her wings when she pushes through the hole to enter the fig. Once she enters, she can never leave again.

FROM SEED TO STRANGLER

After the wasps have done their work, the pollinated flowers produce seeds. Birds and other creatures eat the figs and spread the seeds in their poop.

The sticky seeds land on tree branches. Banyans begin life there as **epiphytes** (EHP-uh-fyts). As banyans grow, they send down roots that wrap around the host and slowly strangle it. When the roots reach the ground, they steal water and nutrients, which are things the host tree needs to stay alive. Over time, the host tree dies.

SEEDS OF KNOWLEDGE

The growing banyan tree also creates a thick canopy that robs the host tree of the sunlight necessary to make food. This plays a part in the host tree's death.

After the host tree dies, it leaves a hollow space inside the banyan tree roots that wrapped around it.

HOW BANYANS GET BIGGER

Banyan trees keep growing, spreading out wider and wider. How are they able to do this? Why don't their huge branches break off? The answer to their almost magical growth is their aerial or prop roots.

As the banyan trees' branches grow, they drop down these sturdy roots. Over time, these roots grow thick until they look like individual tree trunks. The roots support the huge branches, which then grow even longer and send down still more roots.

This looks like a forest, but it's really one banyan tree with many prop roots!

BENEFITS OF THE BANYAN TREE

Banyans aren't just weird, amazing trees. They also provide many benefits. Their figs supply food to people and many kinds of animals. Even the leaves can be eaten!

Banyan wood is sturdy. It is used to build houses and furniture. The bark is used to make paper and rope. And for thousands of years, parts of the banyan tree have been used to make medicine, or a drug to make a sick person well. It can treat everything from pain to major illnesses.

SEEDS OF KNOWLEDGE

The banyan tree holds a special place in the belief systems of Hinduism and Buddhism. It is sometimes called the tree of knowledge or tree of life.

Birds, fruit bats, monkeys, and people eat the bright red, ripe figs. The huge leaves are also used as plates!

OTHER STRANGLER FIGS

As you learned at the beginning of this book, the banyan is a strangler fig. But it's not the only one! About 900 fig species exist, and many are stranglers. They grow in tropical areas around the world.

Like the banyan tree, each strangler is pollinated by only one species of tiny wasp. Each produces figs that feed both people and animals. And stranglers supply food year-round, even when other fruit trees don't. Stranglers are very important plants!

SEEDS OF KNOWLEDGE

Over 1,200 animal species eat figs. In addition to people, that includes almost all known fruit bats and one out of every 10 bird species in the world.

This strangler fig species has great importance to followers of Buddhism and Hinduism.

GLOSSARY

aerial: operating in the air

canopy: the upper branches of a tree or forest

cycle: a series of events that happens over and over again

epiphyte: a plant that grows on another plant and gets water and food from air, rain, and dead plant matter

female: an animal that produces young or lays eggs. Also, a plant that makes seeds.

host: an animal or plant in or on which another animal or plant lives and gets its food or protection

male: an animal that cannot produce young or lay eggs. Also, a plant that does not make seeds.

mate: to come together to make babies

pollinate: to take pollen from one flower, plant, or tree to another

prop: something that is used to support something and keep it in place

sprout: to grow and produce new leaves

trunk: the thick main stem of a tree

FOR MORE INFORMATION

Books

Lawrence, Ellen. *Extreme Trees: And How They Got That Way.* New York, NY: Bearport Publishing Co., 2015.

Spilsbury, Louise, and Richard Spilsbury. *Killer Plants.* Minneapolis, MN: Bellwether Media, Inc., 2017.

Thorogood, Chris. *Perfectly Peculiar Plants.* Lake Forest, CA: Words & Pictures, 2018.

Websites

Banyan Facts for Kids
kids.kiddle.co/Banyan
Discover more about banyan trees and see some great photos on this site.

A Beautiful but Tricky Tree
www.wildernessclassroom.com/a-beautiful-but-tricky-tree/
Learn about strangler figs and the rain forests in which they grow on this website.

See Why Animals Flock to This Tree Every Two Years
bit.ly/2Xj8VSJ
Watch a video from National Geographic about how the fruit of a strangler fig feeds animals of the rain forest.

Publisher's note to educators and parents: Our editors have carefully reviewed these websites to ensure that they are suitable for students. Many websites change frequently, however, and we cannot guarantee that a site's future contents will continue to meet our high standards of quality and educational value. Be advised that students should be closely supervised whenever they access the internet.

INDEX